DATE DUE

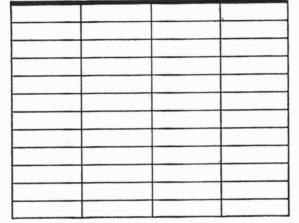

WORLD ALMANAC® LIBRARY OF THE STATES

California

THE GOLDEN STATE

by Scott Ingram

Curriculum Consultant: Jean Craven,
Director of Instructional Support,
Albuquerque, NM, Public Schools

WORLD ALMANAC® LIBRARY

Please visit our web site at: www.worldalmanaclibrary.com
For a free color catalog describing World Almanac® Library's list of high-quality books
and multimedia programs, call 1-800-848-2928 or fax your request to (414) 332-3567.

Library of Congress Cataloging-in-Publication Data

Ingram, Scott (William Scott).
        California, the Golden State / by Scott Ingram.
            p. cm. — (World Almanac Library of the states)
        Includes bibliographical references and index.
        Summary: Illustrations and text present the history, geography, people, politics and
    government, economy, and social life and customs of California, which is the most
    populous of the fifty states.
        ISBN 0-8368-5113-7 (lib. bdg.)
        ISBN 0-8368-5282-6 (softcover)
        1. California—Juvenile literature. [1. California.] I. Title. II. Series.
    F861.3.I54   2002
    979.4—dc21   2001046989

This edition first published in 2002 by
World Almanac® Library
330 West Olive Street, Suite 100
Milwaukee, WI 53212 USA

This edition © 2002 by World Almanac® Library.

Design and Editorial: **Jack&Bill**/Bill SMITH STUDIO Inc.
Editors: Jackie Ball and Kristen Behrens
Art Directors: Ron Leighton and Jeffrey Rutzky
Photo Research and Buying: Christie Silver and Sean Livingstone
Design and Production: Maureen O'Connor and Jeffrey Rutzky
World Almanac® Library Editors: Patricia Lantier, Amy Stone, Valerie J. Weber,
Catherine Gardner, Carolyn Kott Washburne, Alan Wachtel, Monica Rausch
World Almanac® Library Production: Scott M. Krall, Eva Erato-Rudek, Tammy Gruenewald,
Katherine A. Goedheer

Photo credits: p. 5 (top) © PhotoDisc, (bottom) © MapResources; p. 6 (all) © Corel; p. 7 (top)
© PhotoDisc, (bottom) © Corel; p. 9 © Corel; p. 10 © Corel; p. 11 © ArtToday; p. 12
© PhotoDisc; p. 13 © Corel; p. 14 © Dorothea Lange/TimePix; p. 15 © Library of Congress;
p. 17 © Corel; p. 18 © Corel; p. 19 © Corel; p. 20 Carlsbad CVB, © PhotoDisc, Mammoth
Lakes Resort; p. 21 (all) © PhotoDisc; p. 23 © PhotoDisc; p. 26 (left) San Jose CVB; (right)
© PhotoDisc; p. 27 © John Poimiroo; p. 30 © Tom Myers; p. 31 (top left) © Library of
Congress, (top right) © Library of Congress; p. 31 (right) © Lisa Quinones/TimePix; p. 32
© PhotoDisc; p. 33 © Corel; p. 34 (top) San Jose CVB, (bottom) © Corel; p. 35 © PhotoDisc;
p. 37 (top) © Lou Dematteis/TimePix, (bottom) © Mike Blake/TimePix; p. 38 © PhotoDisc;
p. 39 (left) © PhotoDisc, (right) © Artville; p. 40 © Sandy Felsenthal/CORBIS; p. 41 (left) NASA;
(right) © Shaun Best/TimePix; p. 42 © Library of Congress; p. 44 (top) © Corel, (bottom)
courtesy of Los Angeles CVB; p. 45 © Corel

Printed in the United States of America

1 2 3 4 5 6 7 8 9 06 05 04 03 02

California

Come One, Come All

You name it, and California probably has it — and more of it than many other states. Cars. Highways. Mountain ranges. Habitats. And, above all, people. The most populous state in the Union started on its spectacular growth curve in 1849, swelled by hundreds of thousands of "forty-niners" pouring in, drawn by a few famous flakes of gold discovered at Sutter's Mill the year before. The gold rush ended, but the stampede of people never did. During the Great Depression of the 1930s, the Dust Bowl drove another million people westward as they sought a better life. Until 1960 California's population doubled almost every twenty years. In the past forty years, it has tripled. The growth is slower now, but still people come, attracted by the climate and natural beauty, economic opportunity, and the promise — for some — of a relaxed and rewarding lifestyle.

The population is as richly varied as it is huge. In fact, it is a study in cultural diversity — and includes one-fourth of all U.S. immigrants. California is home to the largest populations of U.S. citizens whose ancestors originally came from China, Japan, Korea, the Philippines, and Vietnam. It has the highest population of Native Americans, too. Since California began life as a Spanish territory, and then was ruled by Mexico, it is not surprising that the state's Mexican heritage is strong. California's Latino population makes up approximately one-third of the state's entire populace.

The boundary of two giant sections, or plates, of Earth's crust runs along the California coast. The plates' movement produces earthquakes along six "fault lines" that cut across California. One — the San Andreas — runs almost the entire length of the state. In some places little earthquakes happen almost continually and pretty much harmlessly, but when "Big Ones" hit — as in San Francisco in 1906 and 1989 and near Los Angeles in 1994 — they can cause enormous damage and loss of life. Still, restless settlers seek a restless new home in California.

▶ Map of California, showing the interstate highway system, as well as major towns and waterways.

▶ Map of Los Angeles, showing its freeways and several important tourist sites.

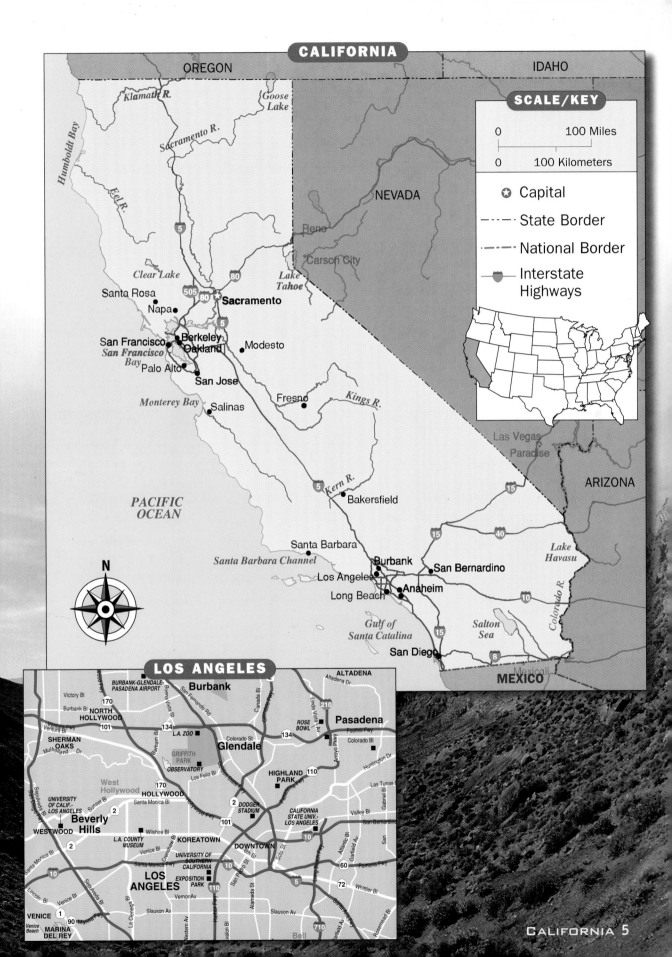

CALIFORNIA

OREGON

IDAHO

NEVADA

Klamath R.

Goose Lake

Sacramento R.

Humboldt Bay

Eel R.

Reno

Carson City

Clear Lake

Lake Tahoe

Santa Rosa

Napa

⭐ Sacramento

San Francisco Berkeley
Oakland
San Francisco Bay
Palo Alto

Modesto

San Jose

Monterey Bay

Salinas

Fresno

Kings R.

PACIFIC OCEAN

Kern R.

Bakersfield

Las Vegas
Paradise

ARIZONA

Lake Havasu

Santa Barbara

Santa Barbara Channel

Burbank
Los Angeles
Long Beach
Anaheim

San Bernardino

Colorado R.

N

Gulf of Santa Catalina

Salton Sea

San Diego

Mexicali

MEXICO

SCALE/KEY

| 0 | 100 Miles |
| 0 | 100 Kilometers |

⭐ Capital

–··–··– State Border

–·–·– National Border

🛡 Interstate Highways

LOS ANGELES

ALTADENA
Altadena Dr

Burbank

BURBANK-GLENDALE-PASADENA AIRPORT

Victory Bl

Burbank Bl

NORTH HOLLYWOOD

Ventura Fwy

SHERMAN OAKS

Mulholland Dr

West Hollywood

HOLLYWOOD

UNIVERSITY OF CALIF.- LOS ANGELES

Sunset Bl

Santa Monica Bl

Beverly Hills

WESTWOOD

Wilshire Bl

L.A. COUNTY MUSEUM

Venice Bl

KOREATOWN

Santa Monica Fwy

LOS ANGELES

UNIVERSITY OF SOUTHERN CALIFORNIA

EXPOSITION PARK

Slauson Av

VENICE

Venice Beach

MARINA DEL REY

San Fernando Rd

Buena Vista St

L.A. ZOO

GRIFFITH PARK

OBSERVATORY

Los Feliz Bl

DODGER STADIUM

Canada Bl

Linda Vista

ROSE BOWL

Pasadena

Foothill Fwy

Colorado St

Glendale

Colorado Bl

HIGHLAND PARK

CALIFORNIA STATE UNIV.- LOS ANGELES

DOWNTOWN

8th St

Soto St

Huntington Dr

Las Tunas

Gabriel Bl

Valley Bl

San Bernardino

Atlantic Av

Garfield Av

San

Pomona Fwy

Whittier Bl

Slauson Av

Rosemead Bl

Bell

Arroyo Pkwy

CALIFORNIA **5**

CALIFORNIA (CA), The Golden State

Entered Union

September 9, 1850 (31st state)

Capital	Population
Sacramento	407,018

Total Population (2000)

33,871,648 (most populous state)

Largest Cities	Population
Los Angeles	3,694,820
San Diego	1,223,400
San Jose	894,493
San Francisco	776,733
Long Beach	461,522

Land Area

155,959 square miles (403,934 square kilometers) (3rd largest state)

State Motto

"Eureka" — *Greek for "I have found it"*

State Song

"I Love You, California," *by F. B. Silverwood*

State Animal

California Grizzly Bear — *The largest of the three types of bears in North America. Today the grizzly bear is on the endangered species list and no longer can be seen in the wild in California.*

State Bird

California Valley Quail

State Fish

Golden Trout — *Native only to California, this fish has now also been raised in other states.*

State Marine Fish

Garibaldi — *This golden orange fish is found in the shallow waters off the coast of southern California.*

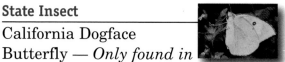

State Insect

California Dogface Butterfly — *Only found in California. The male butterflies have a yellow silhouette on their wings.*

State Tree

California Redwood — *Also called giant sequoias, these are the world's tallest trees and live for hundreds of years. The tallest can measure more than 360 feet (110 meters), making it taller than the Statue of Liberty.*

State Flower

Golden Poppy — *California Native Americans used these flowers as a source of both food and oil.*

State Gem

Benitoite — *An extremely rare gemstone, it ranges in color from light blue to sapphire and occasionally violet.*

State Mineral

Gold — *The discovery of gold in 1848 led to a sharp increase in California's population from 14,000 to 250,000.*

PLACES TO VISIT

Sequoia National Park, *Sierra Nevada*

Here visitors can see unspoiled beauty that rivals sister park Yosemite — but without the crowds. You can walk up to the largest tree on Earth or hike to the highest point in the contiguous United States.

Disneyland, *Anaheim*

The famed theme park, the brainchild of Walt Disney, opened in 1955. Today it is visited by more than fourteen million people each year.

Hollywood, *Los Angeles*

It is a star-studded experience from Hollywood Boulevard to the 50-foot (15-meter) "Hollywood" sign set atop the Hollywood Hills.

For other places and events, see p. 44

BIGGEST, BEST, AND MOST

- The most populous state in the Union.
- More miles of freeway than any other U.S. state.
- Hottest recorded temperature in the United States — Death Valley, 134° Fahrenheit (57° Celsius) on July 10, 1913.
- The location of the world's most fertile valley.
- More national tourism sites than any other state.
- The location of the most active earthquake fault in the world — the San Andreas Fault.

STATE FIRSTS

- The United Nations was founded in San Francisco in 1945.
- In 1948 the first McDonald's opened in San Bernardino. With the help of eight milkshake multimixers, so many people had never been served so fast.
- In that same year the Frisbee, the original flying saucer disc, was invented.

Older Than Methuselah

The high altitudes of California's White Mountains are low on water and oxygen — not the most pleasant place to live. That is where the oldest living tree in the world stands — a 4,700-year-old bristlecone pine. Its exact location is kept a secret.

Scientists counted the tree's rings to find out its age by boring a hole hardly bigger than a needle into its trunk. The boring tool removed a slender section, allowing the age of the tree to be determined.

Game Canceled Due to . . . Earthquakes?

Minutes before Game Three of the 1989 World Series between the Oakland A's and the San Francisco Giants, Mother Nature interrupted. Candlestick Park, San Francisco, shook as an earthquake rocked the San Francisco Bay area and beyond.

San Francisco has been the epicenter of other major quakes, including the devastating 1906 quake, which led to a fire that destroyed the city.

American Paradise

> Know that, on the right hand of the Indies, there is an island called California, very near to the Terrestrial Paradise . . .
> — *Garcia Ordonez de Montalvo, 1510*

Most anthropologists feel that the earliest inhabitants of today's California were already living in the area fifteen to twenty thousand years ago. They spread out across the North and South American continents to form numerous nations and tribes.

The mountain ranges of the Pacific Coast separated Native Americans of California from the cultures in what became Mexico and the western United States. As a result, the Native peoples and societies of California bore little resemblance to the Native Americans of the Great Plains and had no ties of language or culture with them. Native Californians generally lived in large family groups or clans, without the wider organization of the Indian nations to the east.

The lack of rain made agriculture impractical for early Californians, but the mild climate and rich soil allowed them to harvest wild nuts and berries and catch the fish that filled the many streams and rivers flowing from the Sierras. Acorns, ground into flour, were a dietary staple.

A constant food supply, mild climate, and peace resulted in a large, healthy Native population. Historians estimate that when Europeans first came to California, the Native population was probably close to 130,000.

First Contact

Europeans first came to the West Coast in the mid 1530s when Spanish explorer Hernán Cortés's men entered Baja, or lower, California, now part of Mexico. Juan Cabrillo's 1542 expedition landed as far north as Santa Barbara. More than two hundred years passed, however, before Spain established coastal colonies.

Native Americans of California

- Cahuilleno
- Karok
- Modoc
- Mojave
- Paiute
- Pomo
- Wyandot
- Yokuts

An Imaginative Name

The name "California" came from a popular romance novel published in Spain in 1510. The tale told of an island paradise near the Indies ruled by the beautiful Queen Califia and populated by women warriors called Amazons.

In 1769 the first exploration parties traveled north. Spanish soldiers and priests established a *presidio* (fort) and mission at San Diego. By the end of the 1700s, California had a chain of missions as far north as San Francisco, many founded by Father Junipero Serra. Other missions followed, and *pueblos* (small towns) arose near them.

After 1769 most Native Californians came under the control of the mission fathers. The Franciscan monks came to convert Indians to Christianity and teach them the ways of European society. Conversion was often forced, and converts had to live within the walled missions.

By the time the mission system ended in 1834, years of contact with Europeans had decimated the Native population. Spaniards had introduced new diseases to which Native people had no resistance. Crowded, harsh living conditions at the missions contributed to the Indians' health problems. The tribes of the coast, the "Mission Indians," were most affected.

In 1821 Mexico won independence from Spain, and California was part of the new nation. Under Spanish rule, few land grants to individuals had been made. Under Mexican rule, governors granted land for individual *ranchos,* or "ranches." Thus began the ranchero era, when cattle raising drove the region's economy. The rancheros, however, became increasingly dependent on the goods of foreign traders who came in search of hides. As British, Canadian, and American settlers moved to Oregon, many non-Mexicans also came south into northern California.

The first white men to come overland were trappers who arrived in 1826, led by Jedediah Smith. Many thousands were to follow.

In the spring of 1846, rumors of a possible war between

▼ The San Luis Rey Mission in the Oceanside section of San Diego was established by Father Fermin Francisco de Lasuen on June 13, 1798.

Mexico and the United States reached California. U.S. settlers near Sonoma declared California an independent republic. They unfurled a flag featuring a star and a grizzly bear, thus initiating the Bear Flag Revolt. Barely one month later, on July 7, U.S. Commodore John Drake Sloat landed at Monterey, California, and declared the area U.S. territory.

The United States's war with Mexico ended with the signing of the Treaty of Guadalupe Hidalgo on March 10, 1848. California officially became part of the United States in 1850.

The Great Gold Rush

My eye was caught by something shining in the bottom of the ditch.
— James Marshall, 1848

Johann A. Sutter was a Swiss businessman who had received a land grant of 48,000 acres (19,424 hectares) from the Mexican government in 1839. He decided to lay out a town. That required lumber and therefore a sawmill. While deepening the stream chosen to run the sawmill, Sutter's partner, James Marshall, made a spectacular discovery on January 24, 1848. Gold!

It was not until the following May that word reached San Francisco. But then, almost overnight, thousands rushed to the gold fields to stake a claim.

There were no telegraph lines, nor a railroad, so news of the gold strike had to travel by ship to the Atlantic Coast. The ocean journey around the Horn of South America took six or seven months. It wasn't until June 1848 that California's military governor, Colonel Richard Barnes Mason, persuaded President James Polk to officially announce the gold strike in his State of the Union message. The address, delivered on December 5, 1848, triggered a rush of fortune seekers. The "forty-niners" were on their way to California.

Not everyone who came to California during the gold rush planned to wield a pan or pickax in the gold fields. Many understood that there was

Johann Augustus Sutter
1803–1880

Some settlers who crossed the Great Plains to California were led by John Bidwell and John Bartleson in 1841. Bidwell and his group settled in northern California, and Bidwell found work under Johann Sutter. A Swiss businessman, Sutter had come to San Francisco in 1839. The Mexican governor gave Sutter an enormous land grant along the Sacramento and American Rivers, where he established the colony of Nueva Helvetia (New Switzerland). Sutter built a fort that became an important stopover for U.S. settlers, and it was near the fort that gold was found. Unfortunately, although the gold rush brought prosperity to many people, Sutter went bankrupt, in large part because his property was overrun by squatters and settlers. Sutter's original colony of Nueva Helvetia eventually became the city of Sacramento.

money to be made by providing the gold miners with goods and services. The influx of enterprising business people became a steady theme of California history.

As thousands of forty-niners joined the rush, the need for a government became more critical. Congress and the president were slow to act, so in September 1849, forty-eight delegates met in Monterey to draw up a state constitution. The document made California a "free" state that excluded slavery. A year later, on September 9, 1850, President Millard Fillmore signed the bill making California the thirty-first state.

Growth and Expansion

With the discovery of gold, California's population exploded almost overnight. While Johann Sutter had dreamed of a "Sutterville" that would make him rich, squatters overran his property, and the city of Sacramento took root. It served as a trading center and state capital and also became the state's first railroad depot.

Rapid growth, however, could not hide the problems of a "melting pot" society. In the 1850s, as the end of the gold

A Shameful Past

Anti-Chinese feeling spread from the northern mining camps to farming regions and industrial sites throughout the state. After a national depression struck California in the 1870s, the U.S. Congress passed the first Chinese Exclusion Act, barring Chinese immigration for ten years.

▼ An abandoned mining town in the Sierra Nevadas.

boom for independent miners became apparent, white "American" miners became intolerant of other nationalities — especially people of color. In 1850 the new California legislature passed a law charging all non-U.S. citizens $20 per month for a gold-prospecting license. Though the law was repealed the next year, many Chinese left the camps and moved to San Francisco. Soon they had created America's first "Chinatown." Despite the prejudice, many more Chinese came to the "Golden Mountain," as California was known in China. Of the sixty-seven thousand people who came to California in 1852, more than twenty thousand were from China.

The first federal census in California (1860) counted 308,000 residents. Amazingly, the population had almost tripled since 1847. By the mid-1850s cattle ranching was booming. Still, Californians faced the difficulty of transporting goods in and out of the state — a difficulty that would remain until a rail link was completed to the eastern United States. That objective was achieved on May 10, 1869.

Railroads brought large-scale changes to California's economy and population. Along with huge irrigation projects, the new transportation links allowed citrus growing and other large agricultural operations to become critical parts of the state economy. The enormous and enormously fertile Central Valley became one of the world's leading food producers.

Expansion of rail service in California had another important result. Before railroads Los Angeles was a sleepy village. When the Santa Fe Railway gave Los Angeles its own direct line to the East in 1885, the town's population quickly quadrupled.

Also in the 1880s the first campaign to promote California as a vacation paradise began. People with no thought of settling permanently were intrigued by the idea of visiting the state via the new railroads. California soon became a major tourist destination.

Into a New Century

The 1890 census showed that the population of Los Angeles and San Diego had quadrupled in ten years. As newcomers swarmed in, California failed to recognize the needs of groups that had lived there long before the gold

Central Pacific

In January 1863, at the height of the Civil War, work began on the Central Pacific Railroad that was to run from Sacramento and join California with the East. On May 10, 1869, at Promontory Point, Utah, the Central Pacific joined the Union Pacific railroad, completing the first transcontinental railway. This incredible feat could not have been accomplished without Chinese laborers. At one time, more than ten thousand Chinese worked on the line, demonstrating physical courage in laying track and blasting routes through the Sierras. By 1870, sixty-three thousand Chinese lived in the United States, almost all in California.

rush. White Californians ignored legal agreements
with Native Californians that had been established
in Mexican deeds, and Native groups were forced onto
remote and desolate reservations.

In 1846 about 100,000 Californians were Native
Americans and 11,500 of California's 14,000 non-Native
residents were of Spanish or Mexican descent. By 1850
Spanish-speaking Californians were just 15 percent of the
non-Native population; by 1870 only 4 percent. It was not
until their numbers were increased by new Hispanic
immigration in the twentieth century that Latinos would
again play a major role in the state's politics and culture.

The Twentieth Century

Like many Americans in the 1920s and 1930s, Californians
felt as though they were on a roller coaster. The Roaring
Twenties, a decade of economic plenty, was followed by
the thirties and the worst depression in the state's — and
the nation's — history.

Just when things seemed as though they could not get
any worse, drought sucked the farmlands of Oklahoma,
Texas, and Arkansas dry. Wind kicked up monstrous dust
storms that blackened the sky. The states afflicted became

known as the Dust Bowl. Hundreds of thousands of victims of the Dust Bowl in Oklahoma, called "Okies," piled their meager belongings into broken-down cars and headed for the "Golden State." Most Californians did not welcome the newcomers, but they came in huge numbers nevertheless. More than ten thousand arrived every month during the darkest days of the Depression.

With the outbreak of World War II, California became a training area and shipping point for military personnel heading for the war in the Pacific. The defense industry became well established, especially in the shipyards and aircraft manufacturing plants of southern California. Unfortunately, the state's — and the nation's — long history of anti-Asian sentiment also surfaced during the war. More than 110,000 Japanese Americans on the West Coast were removed from their homes and businesses. The 1950s and 1960s saw the further expansion of California's economy into tourism and aerospace. California became a leading manufacturing state for vehicles, satellites, and components.

Hippie Days

The late 1960s saw an expansion of a different kind in California. San Francisco became the center of the so-called hippie movement, a youth rebellion against the adult culture and values of the Vietnam War years. Centered in the Haight-Ashbury neighborhood of San Francisco, the hippie culture became another prominent facet of the California image.

The 1970s witnessed a somewhat darker mood in the Golden State. The gasoline crisis and an economic downturn depressed the state and the nation. For the last twenty years of the twentieth century, California faced many modern versions of its traditional themes. A new boom in computer hardware and software development in the area south of San Francisco now called Silicon Valley brought enormous wealth. At the same time a wave of immigrants from around the world strained its social systems to breaking point, leading once again to old anti-immigrant feelings.

At the dawn of the twenty-first century, California is still a land of wonder and beauty. But it also faces modern problems such as overcrowding, environmental damage, and energy shortages. Just as in the days of the gold rush, California holds equal measures of promise and risk.

Executive Order 9066

In February 1942, President Franklin Roosevelt signed this order, which required all Japanese Americans to be evacuated from the West Coast and confined to internment camps. The camps were set in isolated, inhospitable areas around the country. The barracks where the Japanese Americans lived were hastily built without consideration for climate or privacy. Surrounded by barbed wire and armed guards, the Japanese Americans lived in the camps until the end of the war in 1945. It took nearly forty years, until 1988, for the U.S. government to issue an apology for the internment of these U.S. citizens.

More People Than You Can Imagine

> California, where everybody is born beautiful and nobody grows old.
> — *Inez Haynes Gillmore,* The Californiacs, *1916*

Californians are a mixture of the histories and traditions that make the United States unique. The first European arrivals, from Spain, came to a region that was already populated with an estimated 130,000 Native Americans. Today it has the largest Native population of any state. Of course, California has the largest of a lot of different types of people. The first federal census conducted in California in 1860 counted 308,000 residents. Since then the state's population has grown by a factor of nearly 113 times. The 2000 census counted 33.8 million Californians, making it the most populous state in the nation. California's large population includes people of a wide range of backgrounds, making it one of the most diverse states as well.

A Land of Opportunity

California attracts people from all over the United States and

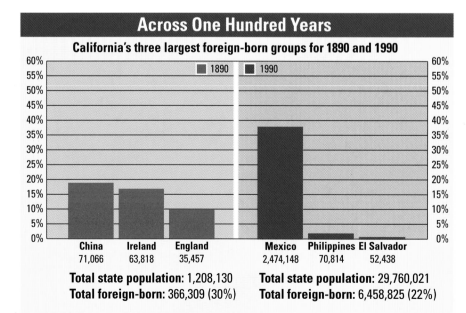

Across One Hundred Years

California's three largest foreign-born groups for 1890 and 1990

■ 1890   ■ 1990

| China 71,066 | Ireland 63,818 | England 35,457 | Mexico 2,474,148 | Philippines 70,814 | El Salvador 52,438 |

Total state population: 1,208,130
Total foreign-born: 366,309 (30%)

Total state population: 29,760,021
Total foreign-born: 6,458,825 (22%)

Patterns of Immigration

The total number of people who immigrated to California in 1998 was 170,126. Of that number, the largest immigrant groups were from Mexico (37%), the Philippines (10%), and China (9%).

◀ Los Angeles is California's largest city and the second largest in the United States. More people of Mexican ancestry live in Los Angeles than any other city in the world except Mexico City.

all over the world. From 1980 to 2000 more than 20 percent of all immigrants to the United States came to California. People are drawn to California because of its promise of economic opportunity, but the huge numbers of immigrants have often created tensions.

Anti-Immigrant Feeling

Since 1850, when laborers in the gold fields were charged $20 a month if they were not U.S. citizens, California's local and state governments have attempted to impose a variety of laws intended to discourage immigration. These included state legislation to restrict Chinese immigrants and an attempt in 1905 to make Japanese children in San Francisco attend separate schools. At the federal level,

Age Distribution in California
(approximate)

0–4	2,486,981
5–19	7,747,590
20–24	2,381,288
25–44	10,714,403
45–64	6,945,728
65 & over	3,595,658

Heritage and Background, California — Year 2000

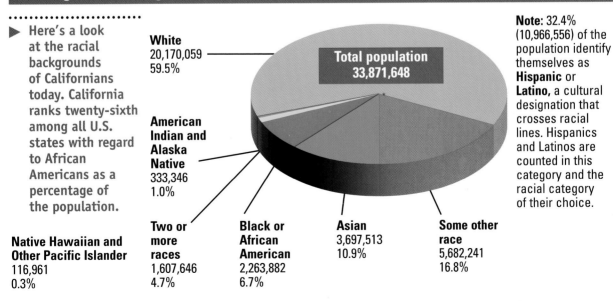

▶ Here's a look at the racial backgrounds of Californians today. California ranks twenty-sixth among all U.S. states with regard to African Americans as a percentage of the population.

White
20,170,059
59.5%

Total population
33,871,648

American Indian and Alaska Native
333,346
1.0%

Native Hawaiian and Other Pacific Islander
116,961
0.3%

Two or more races
1,607,646
4.7%

Black or African American
2,263,882
6.7%

Asian
3,697,513
10.9%

Some other race
5,682,241
16.8%

Note: 32.4% (10,966,556) of the population identify themselves as **Hispanic** or **Latino,** a cultural designation that crosses racial lines. Hispanics and Latinos are counted in this category and the racial category of their choice.

Congress passed Chinese Exclusion Acts and, in 1924, the National Origins Quota Act, which attempted to bar all further immigration from Japan and other Asian countries. All of these laws were eventually overturned.

The latest example of anti-immigrant sentiment showing itself in legislation in California was Proposition 187. This 1994 law attempted to deny public social services, publicly funded health care, and public education to people suspected of being illegal immigrants. The law was declared unconstitutional by California's Supreme Court.

Where They Live

California's population density of about 217 people per square mile (82 people per sq km) is almost three times the national average. Surprisingly, for a state that is third overall in land area, more than 70 percent of Californians live within 10 miles (16 km) of the coast.

Educational Levels of California Workers (age 25 and over)	
Less than 9th grade	2,085,905
9th to 12th grade, no diploma	2,364,623
High school graduate, including equivalency	4,167,897
Some college, no degree or associate degree	5,710,400
Bachelor's degree	2,858,107
Graduate or professional degree	1,508,567

▼ The shore at Oceanside, San Diego, where vacationers and hard-working Californians can relax.

Education

Education has always played an important role in the life of California's citizens. The first state library was established in 1850, the year that California became a state. Today there are more than one thousand public libraries in the state.

The first schools in California's early days were established at Roman Catholic missions to educate Native Americans. Today state law requires children in California to attend school from age six through fifteen. Students who pass a special examination are allowed to leave school or to seek admission to a California community college at age sixteen. Children who have not completed high school or who have not passed the special examination must go to school at least part time until the age of eighteen.

California has almost four hundred two- and four-year colleges and universities. The state has the largest system of state colleges and universities in the United States with more than twenty colleges and universities and an enrollment of more than three hundred thousand students. State law guarantees University of California admission to the top 12 percent of the state's high school graduates, California State University admission to the top third, and a community college seat to all other high school graduates. Tuition in the state system is rated among the most affordable of any system in the country. Enrollment in state institutions of higher learning now stands at 1.3 million, with about seven hundred thousand additional students expected to enroll by 2015.

▲ A street festival at First and Main Streets in Los Angeles.

Religion

Californians are affiliated with many religions. About three-quarters of Californians belong to Christian churches. Between one-quarter and one-third of the population are Catholic, reflecting both the history of Spanish settlement in the state and more recent immigration from Mexico and from Central and South America. Some of the Protestant Christian churches in the state are Baptists, Episcopalians, Methodists, Lutherans, Church of Latter Day Saints, and Presbyterians. Among the many Californians who are not Christian, nearly one million are Jewish. Buddhists make up 0.7 percent of the population and Muslims 0.6 percent. A little more than 1 percent of Californians are agnostic, neither believing nor disbelieving in God.

A State of Amazement

> The greatest surprise to the traveller is that a region which is in perpetual bloom and fruitage, where semi-tropical fruits mature in perfection, and the most delicate flowers dazzle the eye with color the winter through, should have on the whole a low temperature, a climate never enervating, and one requiring a dress of woolen in every month.
> — *Charles Dudley Warner, 1891*

With its picture-postcard coastline, snow-covered peaks, and sun-scorched deserts, California has some of America's most awe-inspiring scenery. In fact, with a land surface of almost 100 million acres (40 million hectares), California has a wider range of geographical regions, landforms, and climates than any area of similar size in the United States.

Climate

California's climates are as diverse as its landscape and differ as much as does southern Ireland from the northern Sahara. Most of the state has two seasons — rainy and dry. The rainy season lasts from October to April in the north and from November to March or April in the south.

The Coast

California's tidal shoreline is 3,427 miles (5,515 kilometers) long, including bays and inlets. California has two great

Nobody's Fault but California's

One of California's most important geographical features is the San Andreas Fault. The Fault is a boundary between two large sections, or plates, of Earth's crust that grind against each other as they move in opposite directions. The greatest recorded movement at one time was nearly 16.5 feet (5 m) in the great San Francisco earthquake of 1906, which is estimated to have measured 8.3 on the Richter Scale.

natural harbors — San Francisco and San Diego Bays. San Francisco Bay covers about 450 square miles (1,166 sq km). It is 200 feet (61 meters) deep at some points. The length of coastline and natural harbors meant that cities, such as San Francisco, developed where ports could be easily built. These ports offered opportunities for trade via shipping and were often the first point of entry for people immigrating in search of a better life.

Many Mountains

The southern California coastal mountains, called the Los Angeles ranges, are between Santa Barbara and San Diego counties. They are also called the Transverse Ranges because they lie in an east–west direction rather than north–south.

The majestic Sierra Nevada Mountain range is located east of the Central Valley and occupies one-fifth of the land in the state. Rushing mountain rivers have cut deep canyons in the western part of the range. The eastern side of the Sierra Nevada Mountains rises steeply, whereas the western side has a more gentle slope. Forests of pine, fir, and cedar cover the lower elevations. Several modern highways that cross the range are usually closed in the winter due to heavy snows.

The Cascade Range extends north from the Sierra Nevadas. Unlike other California ranges, the Cascades were formed by volcanoes. Lassen Peak, which is 10,457 feet (3,187 m) tall, is still active. The Basin and Range Region of the Cascades are part of a larger range that extends into Nevada, Oregon, and Idaho.

Islands

Two groups of islands are located along the California coast. The small, rocky Farallon Islands rise from the ocean about

Death Valley

Death Valley is a deep depression about 130 miles (209 km) long and 6 to 14 miles (10–22 km) wide. At 282 feet (86 m) below sea level, the valley's center is the lowest point in the Western Hemisphere. Death Valley got its ominous name from a band of 49ers who struggled through the region. In the 1880s, the Harmony Borax Company became famous for using twenty-mule teams to haul borax, a mineral used in cleaning products, out of the valley. The region was declared a national park in 1933.

▼ *From left to right:* **Carlsbad Beach; Fanette Island, Lake Tahoe; Mammoth Mountain; coastal scenery; Death Valley; Big Basin Redwoods State Park.**

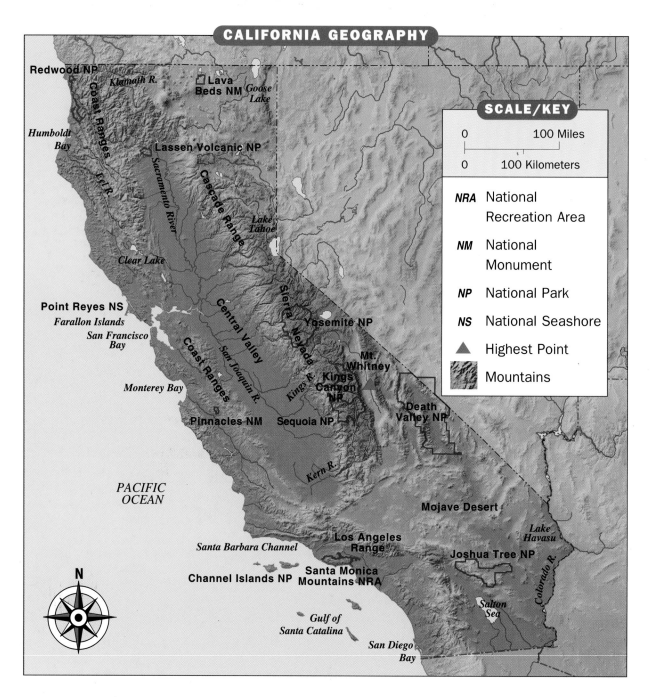

CALIFORNIA GEOGRAPHY

Redwood NP
Klamath R.
Lava Beds NM
Goose Lake
Humboldt Bay
Coast Ranges
Lassen Volcanic NP
Eel R.
Sacramento River
Cascade Range
Lake Tahoe
Clear Lake
Point Reyes NS
Farallon Islands
San Francisco Bay
Central Valley
Sierra Nevada
Yosemite NP
Coast Ranges
San Joaquin R.
Mt. Whitney
Kings R.
Kings Canyon NP
Monterey Bay
Pinnacles NM
Sequoia NP
Death Valley NP
Kern R.
PACIFIC OCEAN
Mojave Desert
Lake Havasu
Santa Barbara Channel
Los Angeles Range
Joshua Tree NP
Colorado R.
Channel Islands NP
Santa Monica Mountains NRA
Salton Sea
N
Gulf of Santa Catalina
San Diego Bay

SCALE/KEY

| 0 | 100 Miles |
| 0 | 100 Kilometers |

NRA National Recreation Area
NM National Monument
NP National Park
NS National Seashore
▲ Highest Point
Mountains

30 miles (48 km) west of San Francisco. The eight Channel Islands lie scattered off the coast of southern California. Catalina is the best known and attracts many vacationers.

Rivers and Valleys

Once an inland sea, California's Central Valley lies between the Coast and Sierra Nevada ranges. More than 400 miles (644 km) long and about 50 miles (80 km) wide, the Central Valley is the most productive agricultural area in the state.

Highest Elevation
Mt. Whitney
14,494 feet
(4,418 meters)

Lowest Elevation
Death Valley
282 feet (86 m) below sea level

The Central Valley is really two valleys in one. The San Joaquin River drains the San Joaquin Valley in the south. The Sacramento River drains the Sacramento Valley in the north. These two rivers, California's longest, are the lifeblood of the Central Valley. Smaller rivers, such as the Feather and the Mokelumne, begin in the eastern mountains and flow west into the Sacramento River, which flows for 400 miles (644 km) through the heart of the valley.

Meanwhile, the Colorado River forms the border in the desert region between southern California and Arizona. In addition to irrigating farmlands, the Colorado is an important source of water for Los Angeles and other cities of southern California.

The Desert

In southern California lies a large, triangular-shaped desert, which is a vast expanse of sandy valleys, dry lake beds, and short, rugged mountain ranges. California's largest desert is the Mojave. It covers 25,000 square miles (58,000 sq km) and was formed millions of years ago when active volcanoes erupted, depositing layers of lava, mud, and ash.

The Colorado Desert stretches over 4,000 square miles (10,360 sq km) in southeastern California. Almost 250 feet (76 m) below sea level, it is part of a great depression that extends southward to the Gulf of California in Mexico. Irrigation with water diverted from the Colorado River has made several valleys in the region suitable for raising crops.

California's Lakes

California has more than eight thousand lakes. Lake Tahoe, in the Sierra Nevada range on the California-Nevada border, is the deepest, with an average depth of about 1,500 feet (427 m). Most lakes east of the Sierras contain dissolved minerals washed down from the mountains. Potash, salt, and other minerals are taken from Owens Lake, Searles Lake, and other dry or partly dry lakes in this region.

The Sierra Club

With so much natural beauty, and so many people coming to enjoy it, it is no surprise that a strong conservation movement thrives in California. In 1892 naturalist John Muir led his fellow conservationists in the founding of the Sierra Club. Californians pressured the Federal government to put Yosemite Valley and nearby giant sequoia groves under protection as a park. Muir's dream for the creation of Yosemite National Park became a reality in 1890.

Making a Living in California

> It used to be said that you had to know what was happening in America because it gave us a glimpse of the future. Today, the rest of America, and after that, Europe, had better heed what happens in California, for it already reveals the type of civilization that is in store for all of us.
>
> — *Alistair Cooke, 1968*

I f California were a separate country, it would have one of the largest economies in the world — larger than that of Brazil, Mexico, or Canada. California produces $1.2 trillion worth of goods and services a year, 13 percent of the U.S. total.

California's population boomed when settlers came searching for gold. Though the gold rush didn't "pan out" for many immigrants, California offered a wealth of economic opportunities. Timber, fishing, livestock, and agriculture were enormous sources of wealth in the state's early economy. The main problem California's economy faced during its first years of statehood was transportation of goods. In the second half of the nineteenth century, the completion of railroad lines connecting the eastern states with northern and southern California opened new doors for the state's economic development.

Industry

The service industry is responsible for almost one-fourth of California's economy. The service field includes jobs in computer and software design, motion picture production, engineering, and legal work. Service jobs also include positions such as child care, landscaping, and restaurant and hotel work.

The next largest areas are finance, trade, and manufacturing. These areas include such activities

Top Employers (of workers age sixteen and over)	
Services	40.9%
Wholesale and retail trade	20.8%
Manufacturing	16.8%
Government workers	14%
Transportation, communications, and other public utilities	6.5%
Construction	6%
Agriculture, forestry, and fisheries)	3%
Mining	2%

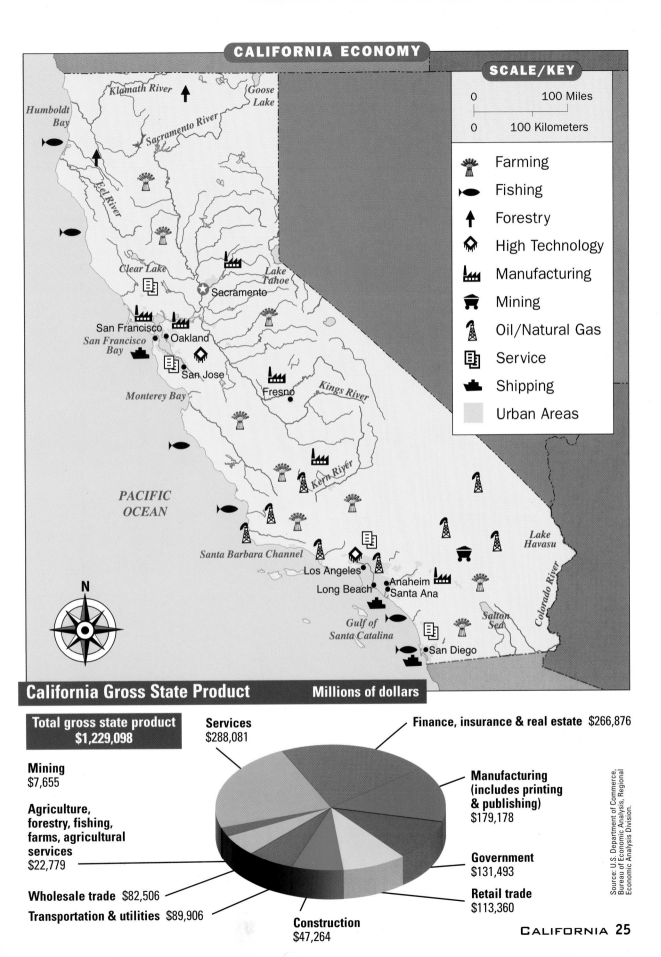

CALIFORNIA ECONOMY

SCALE/KEY

0 — 100 Miles
0 — 100 Kilometers

- Farming
- Fishing
- Forestry
- High Technology
- Manufacturing
- Mining
- Oil/Natural Gas
- Service
- Shipping
- Urban Areas

Klamath River
Goose Lake
Humboldt Bay
Sacramento River
Eel River
Clear Lake
Lake Tahoe
Sacramento
San Francisco
Oakland
San Francisco Bay
San Jose
Monterey Bay
Fresno
Kings River
Kern River
PACIFIC OCEAN
Santa Barbara Channel
Los Angeles
Long Beach
Anaheim
Santa Ana
Lake Havasu
Colorado River
Gulf of Santa Catalina
Salton Sea
San Diego

N

California Gross State Product — Millions of dollars

Total gross state product $1,229,098

- **Services** $288,081
- **Finance, insurance & real estate** $266,876
- **Mining** $7,655
- **Manufacturing (includes printing & publishing)** $179,178
- **Agriculture, forestry, fishing, farms, agricultural services** $22,779
- **Government** $131,493
- **Wholesale trade** $82,506
- **Retail trade** $113,360
- **Transportation & utilities** $89,906
- **Construction** $47,264

San Jose, capital of Silicon Valley, is California's third and the United States's eleventh largest city.

as banking, financing, and the manufacture and sale of high-tech products such as computers.

Toward the end of the twentieth century, California's computer-related service industries prospered. The industries in this field include the development of computer systems, software, and Internet products. Job growth in these fields soared in the 1990s before slumping at the beginning of the twenty-first century.

Agriculture

California is by far the largest agricultural producer in the United States. With more than $25 billion in sales, California makes up roughly one-eighth of U.S. total sales. California's total was greater than the next two states — Texas and Iowa — combined. The largest sales are in dairy products, greenhouse products, and cattle. More than 70 percent of the lettuce in American salads comes from California farms. California also produces more than 90 percent of the grapes and 75 percent of the strawberries that are sold in U.S. stores. California is also the main producer of specialty crops such as kiwis, artichokes, brussels sprouts, and pumpkins.

Made in California

Leading farm products and crops

Milk and dairy products
Grapes
Cotton
Flowers
Oranges
Rice
Hay
Tomatoes
Lettuce
Strawberries
Almonds
Asparagus
Livestock (cattle, sheep, hogs, chickens)

Other products

Electronic and electrical equipment
Computers
Industrial machinery
Transportation equipment and instruments

Foreign Trade

A large part of California's economy — more than 10 percent — depends on foreign trade. The state exports more than $125 billion worth of goods to countries around the world. High-tech products from the electronics, computer, and aerospace industries make up the majority of exports. California's three largest trading partners are Mexico, Japan, and Canada.

Movies and More

As California continued to grow during the early twentieth century, agriculture became dominant in the economy. The cultivation of citrus fruits, mainly oranges and lemons, spread throughout the southern part of the state. The Napa Valley and other areas of northern California are major wine-producing regions.

The discovery of petroleum resources in southern and central California contributed to the oil boom of the 1920s. That decade also saw the beginning of California's connection with the car. Automobiles became part of the "California" lifestyle.

The greatest marketers of this new "golden" life, of course, were motion pictures that were produced locally and distributed globally. The movies discovered California in the early years of the twentieth century, and the film industry soon became a mainstay of the state's economy. Hollywood and nearby locales offered a superior climate and a great variety of landscapes.

From Gelbfisz to Goldwyn

Schmuel Gelbfisz, a Polish Jew from Warsaw, was just one of many who fled Europe seeking freedom from persecution.

Gelbfisz arrived in California in 1913 and changed his name to Samuel Goldfish. There he founded one of the first motion picture companies on the West Coast. He partnered with Edgar and Archibald Selwyn and from them took a new "American" name. He combined the first syllable of his old name, Goldfish, with the last syllable of his partners' name, Selwyn, to get Goldwyn. In 1925 Goldwyn and another European immigrant, Louis B. Mayer, joined forces and formed Metro-Goldwyn-Mayer. MGM Studios was the leading movie studio in Hollywood for more than thirty years.

Geography and Economy

Today California can be divided into five regions with separate economic strengths.

Region	Current Jobs	Industries
Southern California	8 million	Manufacturing, motion pictures, tourism, trade
San Francisco Area	3.5 million	High-tech manufacturing, software development, tourism
Central Valley	2.4 million	Agriculture, manufacturing, financial services, trade
Central Coast	0.7 million	Agriculture, high-tech manufacturing, tourism
Rest of state	0.3 million	Agriculture, forestry, tourism

A Step Ahead

> Congress having failed at its recent session to provide a new government for this country to replace that which existed on the annexation of California to the United States, the undersigned would call attention to the means which he deems best calculated to avoid the embarrassments of our present position.
>
> — B. Riley, Brevet Brigadier General of the United States and Governor of California, June 3, 1849

California, the thirty-first state, was admitted to the Union on September 9, 1850. Before it became a state, California was under a military government, which adopted the state's first constitution in 1849 when the federal government failed to provide a framework for the state's organization. The current constitution was adopted in 1879 (only men were allowed to vote at the time). Since then the California Constitution has been amended more than 350 times.

The California Constitution divides the state government into three branches: executive, legislative, and judicial. The California Constitution also has special provisions regarding the proposal and enactment of laws.

Elected Posts in the Executive Branch

Office	Length of Term	Term Limits
Governor	4 years	2 terms
Lieutenant Governor	4 years	None
Secretary of State	4 years	None
Attorney General	4 years	None
Treasurer	4 years	None
Controller	4 years	None
Insurance Commissioner	4 years	None
Superintendent of Public Instruction	4 years	None

Executive Branch

California's governor is elected to a four-year term and can serve only two terms. Other elected officials in the executive branch are the lieutenant governor, secretary of state, attorney general, treasurer, controller, insurance commissioner, and superintendent of public instruction. Voters also elect the five-member State Board of Equalization, which oversees tax laws.

Legislative Branch

California's legislative branch consists of a senate and an assembly. California's Senate has forty members, each representing about eight hundred thousand people.

Regular sessions of the legislature last two years. They begin on the first Monday in December of each even-numbered year and end on November 30 of the next even-numbered year. The governor may call special sessions at which the legislature can deal only with subjects specified by the governor. There is no time limit on special legislative sessions. The legislature's main responsibilities are to finance state government, pass laws, and provide sessions for discussion of public issues and concerns.

Judicial Branch

As with the federal government, the state supreme court is the highest court in California's judicial system. California Supreme Court justices — one chief justice and six associate justices — are appointed for twelve-year terms. The governor appoints the justices, who are

◀ The California State Capitol building in Sacramento was built in 1860.

How the Oregon System Works

A supporter must collect valid signatures equalling a percentage of the votes cast in the previous gubernatorial election. The measure can then be put on the ballot during the next state election. If the voters approve the measure, it becomes law.

Signatures required for:

• A new law: 5%

• A constitutional amendment: 8%

In a process called the referendum, people can challenge most laws passed by the legislature.

• Signatures required for a referendum: 5%

confirmed by a commission on judicial appointments. The appointments are also confirmed by the public at the next general election. Justices who wish to continue on the bench can be reelected.

Below the supreme court are an appeals court as well as county and local municipal courts. California has six appeal court districts, each with at least one division.

The Oregon System

By the late 1800s California's great natural resources and economic opportunities had provided great wealth and power to a few men who ran lumber, rail, and shipping industries. Some who served in the state government tended to listen more closely to the wealthy. To give more power to the average citizen, California adopted the Oregon System, which permits more direct control by citizens. The Oregon System is named for the first state to adopt it. Today any California resident of any age may suggest an idea for a new law.

General Assembly			
House	Number of Members	Length of Term	Term Limits
Senate	40 senators	4 years	none
Assembly	80 representatives	2 years	none

The White House via California

Two Californians have served as president of the United States

RICHARD MILHOUS NIXON (1969–1974). The only California native to be elected president was Richard Milhous Nixon, born in Yorba Linda, near Los Angeles.

Nixon, a Republican, served two terms in the U.S. House of Representatives beginning in 1946, as senator from 1950–1953, and then two terms as vice president under Dwight D. Eisenhower. After losing the 1960 presidential election to John F. Kennedy, he again won the Republican nomination in 1968 and was elected as the thirty-seventh president.

Months into Nixon's second term, scandal struck. During the 1972 presidential campaign, the offices of the Democratic National Committee were broken into. The crime was traced to officials of the Committee to Re-elect the President. Nixon denied any personal involvement, but tape recordings indicated that he was involved in a cover-up.

On August 8, 1974, faced with what seemed almost certain impeachment, Nixon announced that he would resign. One month later, on September 8, Gerald Ford pardoned Nixon.

RONALD REAGAN (1981–1989)

Although a native of Illinois, Ronald Reagan's political career began in California. The well-known movie actor served as governor of California from 1967 to 1975. In 1980 he was elected the fortieth president and served two terms.

Local Government

California has about 470 incorporated cities. The state constitution gives every city of three thousand five hundred or more people the right to draw up and adopt its own charter. This right is often called home rule. About eighty California cities operate under home-rule charters.

California also has government at the county level. Most of the fifty-eight counties have a form of government that includes a five-member board of supervisors and a number of elected executive officials. Elected officials include an assessor, auditor, clerk, coroner, district attorney, sheriff, superintendent of schools, and treasurer.

▲ Demonstrators protesting Proposition 209, which ended affirmative action in state universities.

Golden Opportunities

> At night thousands of names and slogans are outlined in neon, and searchlight beams often pierce the sky, perhaps announcing a motion picture premiere, perhaps the opening of a hamburger stand.
> — *Philip Van Doren Stern, 1939*

There is so much to do outside in California that it is hard to imagine being indoors — except that there is so much to do inside, too! Name your sport and you can play it or watch it in California. Fishing, diving, surfing, skiing, and mountain biking are just some of the activities people enjoy in California.

The Great Outdoors

California's 18 national forests, 8 national parks, and 260 state parks offer hiking, camping, and wildlife viewing. The Sierra Nevadas of eastern California offer some of the best skiing in the United States, as well as fishing and mountain biking in warmer months. Yosemite National Park is among the most-visited national parks in the country, and one look at the incredible cliffs, waterfalls, and conifer forests will tell you why.

The state's northern region offers eye-pleasing drives along twisting, rugged roads. Farms, redwood forests, and rolling hills offer picture-postcard beauty.

Moving east, toward Sacramento and gold country, travelers can visit museums, ghost towns, and abandoned mines from the state's early days. Some may

The World's Tallest Residents

California's north coast is the only environment in the world that can support the mighty coast redwood. The right mix of longitude, climate, and elevation restricts the giant redwoods' range. These ideal conditions have existed for some time — the redwoods go back twenty million years in their present range. Redwoods can reach ages of two thousand years and regularly reach six hundred years. Incredibly, the mighty coast redwoods grow from seeds no bigger than those of a tomato. These natural skyscrapers may reach heights of over 360 feet (121 m) and have widths reaching 22 feet (7 m) at the base.

TOUR THRU TREE
KLAMATH,CA

even want to pan for their own gold in one of the many rivers flowing through the region. There is still some left — although not much — in the hills.

Heading down the Central Valley brings visitors to the nation's main food-producing regions and to the many "world vegetable capitals" with museums dedicated to lettuce, carrots, onions, and other foods.

The coastal region between San Francisco and Los Angeles contains some of the most spectacular ocean views on the West Coast. Driving along the Pacific Coast Highway, lucky sightseers might spot migrating gray whales heading through ocean waters.

Southern California offers the classic California surfing beaches of Malibu, Venice, Huntington, Redondo, and others. The giant ocean liner *Queen Mary* is docked in Long Beach for visitors to enjoy. Farther south the San Diego area has more beaches, diving, fishing, and possibly the best year-round climate in the United States.

▼ A contestant in a surfing contest at Huntington Beach.

See the Cities

Not all of California's beauty and fun are to be found in nature however. The San Francisco Bay area has long been a tourist magnet. Cable cars carry riders up and down the steep hills of the city from the magnificent gold rush hotels and Union Square to Fisherman's Wharf on the bay. The graceful Golden Gate Bridge spans the bay at its neck. From Chinatown to Golden Gate Park — a scenic area overlooking the Pacific — the city by the bay is one of the most beautiful anywhere. In the center of San Francisco Bay stands Alcatraz Island, once a prison for the nation's most dangerous criminals, now a museum.

▲ The heir to the Winchester gun fortune created a bizarre house with 160 rooms. Today it is a tourist attraction.

▼ Golden Gate Bridge.

South of San Francisco is Los Angeles, which attracts twenty-four million vacationers every year. It is the home of Hollywood and the famed Hollywood Boulevard, where you can "see all the stars." It's possible to take tours of some of the major studios' movie lots, too. Disneyland is in nearby Anaheim. There is more to L.A. than movies — the city has upward of eighty stage theaters and three hundred museums, more than any other U.S. city.

Further south is San Diego. The world-famous San Diego Zoo is one of the most popular destinations in the San Diego region. The 100-acre (40.5-ha) zoo is also a lush botanical garden. Among the San Diego Zoo's four thousand animals, representing eight hundred species, are such favorites as lions, tigers, bears, elephants, giraffes, orangutans, zebras, and gorillas. Most inhabitants live in enclosures that resemble the animals' natural homes in the wild as much as possible. San Diego's ideal climate makes it possible for most of the animals to live outdoors year-round. The zoo is also home to some of the rarest wildlife in the world, including giant pandas and koalas.

▲ A San Francisco cable car and, in the distance, San Francisco Bay and Alcatraz prison, now a major tourist attraction.

Another of California's justly famous tourist attractions is the so-called Hearst Castle. In 1865 George Hearst, a wealthy miner, purchased 40,000 acres (16,194 ha) of ranchland. In 1919 his only son, William Randolph Hearst, owner and publisher of the *San Francisco Examiner* newspaper, inherited the land from his mother. For a number of years, the Hearst family used the land for camping. Finally, Hearst told architect Julia Morgan that he wanted to "build a little something" because he was tired of camping. By then the ranch had grown to more than 250,000 acres (101,214 ha).

Hearst and Morgan's "little something" became one of the world's greatest showplaces. As they planned and built his dream home, Hearst renamed the rocky perch from which it rose *La Cuesta Encantada,* or "The Enchanted

Hill." By 1947 Hearst and Morgan had created an estate of 165 rooms —including sixty-one bathrooms, forty-one fireplaces, and 127 acres (51 ha) of gardens, terraces, pools, and walkways. The estate's magnificent thirty-eight-bedroom main house, *Casa Grande,* and three guest houses are of the Mediterranean style, while the towers of Casa Grande were inspired by a Spanish cathedral.

Sport	Team	Home
Baseball	Anaheim Angels	Edison Field, Anaheim
	Los Angeles Dodgers	Dodger Stadium, Los Angeles
	Oakland Athletics	Network Associates Coliseum, Oakland
	San Diego Padres	Qualcomm Stadium, San Diego
	San Francisco Giants	Pacific Bell Park, San Francisco
Basketball	Golden State Warriors	The Arena in Oakland, Oakland
	Los Angeles Clippers	Staples Arena, Anaheim
	Los Angeles Lakers	Staples Arena, Anaheim
	Sacramento Kings	ARCO Arena, Sacramento
Women's Basketball	Los Angeles Sparks	Staples Arena, Anaheim
	Sacramento Monarchs	ARCO Arena, Sacramento
Football	Oakland Raiders	Network Associates Coliseum, Oakland
	San Diego Chargers	Qualcomm Stadium, San Diego
	San Francisco 49ers	3Com Park, San Francisco
Hockey	Anaheim Mighty Ducks	Arrowhead Pond, Anaheim
	Los Angeles Kings	Staples Arena, Anaheim
	San Diego Gulls	San Diego Sports Arena, San Diego
	San Jose Sharks	Compaq Center, San Jose
Soccer	Los Angeles Galaxy	Rose Bowl, Los Angeles
	San Diego Sockers	San Diego Sports Arena, San Diego
	San Jose Earthquakes	Spartan Stadium, San Jose

Sights to See

Even during the worst economic times in the nation's history, Californians could look proudly on certain accomplishments. Completed in 1935 the Hoover Dam, on the Colorado River, brought water and electric power to thousands of square miles of southern California. In the north the challenge of bridging the San Francisco Bay was successfully met with the completion of the San Francisco-Oakland Bay Bridge in 1936 and the Golden Gate Bridge in 1937.

The San Francisco 49ers battle the St. Louis Rams at 3Com Park.

Los Angeles Laker Kobe Bryant charges to the basket.

Spectator Sports

California has more professional sports teams than any other state — and successful ones, too. Few teams in professional sports can claim the successes of the San Francisco 49ers of the National Football League (NFL) or the Los Angeles Lakers of the National Basketball Association (NBA). In recent years both teams won multiple championships. The 49ers won five Super Bowls in the 1980s and 1990s. The Lakers, led by Hall of Famers Kareem Abdul-Jabbar and Magic Johnson, won five NBA championships the 1980s. In 2000 and 2001 Shaquille O'Neal and Kobe Bryant led the Lakers to two more NBA titles.

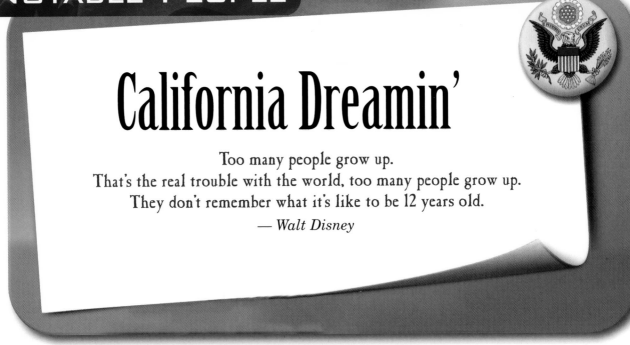

California Dreamin'

Too many people grow up.
That's the real trouble with the world, too many people grow up.
They don't remember what it's like to be 12 years old.

— *Walt Disney*

Following are only a few of the thousands who were born, died, or spent most of their lives in California while making extraordinary contributions to the state and the nation.

WILLIAM RANDOLPH HEARST
NEWSPAPER PUBLISHER

BORN: *April 29, 1863, San Francisco*
DIED: *August 14, 1951, Beverly Hills*

The son of the industrialist and politician George Hearst, Hearst took over his father's newspaper, the San Francisco Examiner, in 1887. By 1927 he controlled a chain of twenty-five newspapers published in major cities throughout the United States. Eventually his magazine properties included Cosmopolitan, Good Housekeeping, Harper's Bazaar, and Town and Country. In 1911 Hearst also began producing newsreels, news segments that were shown in theaters before the feature movie began. He later began producing motion pictures as well. The extent to which he controlled the news media meant that he could exert a powerful influence on public opinion. Reports in his newspapers about Spain's activities in Cuba played a role in the United States's decision to declare war on Spain in 1898. Hearst's papers also helped to achieve social and political reforms. Hearst also had political ambitions and served in the U.S. House of Representatives, though his media empire was his greatest achievement.

JACK LONDON
AUTHOR

BORN: *January 12, 1876, San Francisco*
DIED: *November 22, 1916, Glenn Ellen*

John Griffith London was twenty-one when he joined the 1897 Alaskan gold rush. When he returned to San

Francisco several years later, he began to write about his experiences. His first collection of short stories, The Son of the Wolf, was published in 1900. He continued to write short stories and novels, the most famous of which is The Call of the Wild (1903). Much of his work was inspired by his experiences in the wilderness. The themes he explored and his crisp writing style helped make his books enduring classics.

MARY PICKFORD

ACTRESS AND STUDIO EXECUTIVE

BORN: *April 9, 1893, Toronto, Canada*
DIED: *May 28, 1979, Santa Monica*

Born Gladys Mary Smith, Pickford changed her name like many actors and actresses. She had a long and successful acting career, beginning at age five in Toronto. Later she moved to become a star in New York City. When the motion picture industry began, she became one of the first female movie stars. Pickford was not only an actress but a businesswoman. Her stardom was in large part brought about by her creation of Mary Pickford Studios — an unusual and unusually successful endeavor for a woman living at that time. In 1919 Pickford, producer D. W. Griffith, and actors Charlie Chaplin and Douglas Fairbanks (Pickford's husband from 1920 to 1937) founded the United Artists Corporation. The powerful movie studio produced such films as Charlie Chaplin's The Gold Rush (1925), The African Queen (1951), and The Magnificent Seven (1960).

WALT DISNEY

CARTOONIST AND VISIONARY

BORN: *December 5, 1901, Chicago, IL*
DIED: *December 15, 1966, Los Angeles*

In 1923 twenty-two-year-old Walter Elias Disney began to produce animated motion pictures in Hollywood in partnership with his brother, Roy O. Disney. With their 1928 invention of Steamboat Willie (the original Mickey Mouse), Disney's fame was assured. Disney went on to create the legendary theme park Disneyland in California, as well as the Walt Disney Company, which has been an enduring Hollywood success story. Over Disney's lifetime he produced movies, television shows, comic strips, and more. He produced such classic feature-length animated films as Snow White and the Seven Dwarfs (1937) and Bambi (1942). His legacy lives on today.

DAVE BRUBECK

MUSICIAN

BORN: *December 26, 1920, Concord*

At age four David Warren Brubeck began to play on one of the five pianos his family owned. The early experimentation eventually led to the creation of one of the most successful jazz groups, the Dave Brubeck Quartet, formed in 1951. Brubeck was the group's pianist and composer, and his musical compositions are noted for incorporating classical music devices. The group's most popular album, *Time Out*, has sold millions of copies, and Brubeck has performed for four U.S. presidents — Kennedy, Johnson, Reagan, and Clinton.

SHIRLEY TEMPLE
ACTRESS AND POLITICIAN

BORN: *April 23, 1928, Santa Monica*

Shirley Temple, an internationally famous child star of her day, starred in dozens of movies during the 1930s, including Little Miss Marker (1934) and Heidi (1937). Known for her head of curls (her mother insisted that there always be exactly thirty-six) and her ability to sing and dance, she was a top box office draw during the Great Depression. As an adult, Shirley Temple Black became active in politics and ran unsuccessfully for the U.S. Congress. In 1974, however, she was appointed U.S. ambassador to Ghana and held the post for two years. In 1976 President Gerald R. Ford appointed her to serve as chief of protocol, the first woman in U.S. history to do so. She held the post for two years.

▼ Dick and Mac McDonald had a successful restaurant in San Bernardino that served burgers, fries, and shakes. This eatery was so successful that Ray Kroc thought a whole chain of restaurants might be possible. This is the "Original McDonald's" sign in Des Plaines, Illinois, where Kroc opened his first licensed franchise.

DICK MCDONALD
ENTREPRENEUR

BORN: *February 16, 1909, Manchester, NH*
DIED: *July 14, 1998, Manchester, NH*

MAC MCDONALD
ENTREPRENEUR

BORN: *November 26, 1902, Manchester, NH*
DIED: *December 11, 1971, Palm Springs, CA*

Richard and Maurice McDonald had a simple dream — to be millionaires by the time they were fifty. In the late 1920s, during the Great Depression, elder brother Mac left New Hampshire for California. Upon graduating from high school, Dick followed him. They started out working in the props department at Columbia Studios, but after World War II they opened up their first restaurant in San Bernardino. Although the restaurant was fairly successful, the brothers were sure they could do better. In the process of making their restaurant as efficient as possible, they invented fast food. By 1952 restaurants owned by the McDonalds were a huge success. A year later, they expanded to Phoenix, Arizona, and in that same year, Dick came up with the idea for the world-famous golden arches. In 1961 the brothers sold the restaurant franchise for $2.7 million to Ray Kroc, a salesman from Illinois.

SALLY RIDE
ASTRONAUT
BORN: *May 26, 1951, Encino*

Sally Kristen Ride, the first woman in the U.S. space program to take part in an orbital mission, was also one of the first six women to graduate from the National Aeronautics and Space Administration (NASA) space program. As a mission specialist aboard the space shuttle *Challenger,* Ride took part in launching two satellites and retrieving a third. That was not Ride's only trip into space, however. She also took part in the thirteenth shuttle mission (October 13–15, 1984). Today Ride is the director of the California Space Institute at the Scripps Institution of Oceanography and professor of physics at the University of California at San Diego.

TIGER WOODS
ATHLETE
BORN: *December 30, 1975, Cypress*

Coached by his father, Eldrick "Tiger" Woods began playing golf before the age of two. At the age of six, he entered his first international junior competition, and Woods's career has been a success ever since. In 1991, at age fifteen, he was the youngest person to ever win the U.S. Junior Amateur title. He won the following two years as well. In 1994 he became the youngest player, and the first African American, to win both the U.S. Junior and U.S. Amateur titles. He followed this winning streak by capturing the U.S. Amateur title in 1995 and 1996 as well. To date he has had more than two dozen Professional Golf Association (PGA) victories, as well as four international victories. He shows no signs of stopping.

◀ Sally Ride.

California
History At-A-Glance

1781
Los Angeles is founded; a small band of eleven founding families are of European, African, and Native American heritage.

1848
Gold is discovered.

1908
The first motion picture begins production in California.

1933–34
The first mass-produced commercial aircraft is built in Santa Monica.

1530s
Hernan Cortés explores lower California; region is named.

1850
Statehood is granted and California becomes the 31st state. Four years later the state capital moves from Benicia to Sacramento.

1869
Rail service connects California to the East.

1930s
Dust Bowl spurs immigration; brings 10,000 new settlers per month by 1938.

1769
California is settled by Spain.

1821
California comes under Mexican rule.

1906
Great earthquake and fire in San Francisco.

1935
Statewide irrigation system is begun.

1600   **1700**   **1800**

1492
Christopher Columbus comes to New World.

1607
Capt. John Smith and three ships land on Virginia coast and start first English settlement in New World — Jamestown.

1754–63
French and Indian War.

1776
Declaration of Independence adopted July 4.

1787
U.S. Constitution is written.

1773
Boston Tea Party.

1777
Articles of Confederation adopted by Continental Congress.

1812–14
War of 1812.

United States
History At-A-Glance

1937
Golden Gate Bridge completed.

1942–45
More than 100,000 Japanese Americans in California are sent to internment camps during World War II.

1955
Disneyland opens.

1962
California becomes the most populous state in the Union; between 1940 and 1962, the state's population rose from 9 to 22 million.

1965
Watts riots in Los Angeles, a major race riot in the United States.

1965
Immigration reform law ends quota system and allows large-scale entry of Asians.

1967
The hippie movement reaches its peak; many lived in the Haight-Ashbury area of San Francisco.

1969
Richard Nixon takes office, only California native to be elected president.

1989
Bay Area World Series between Oakland A's and San Francisco Giants is disrupted by massive earthquake centered near Loma Prieta in northern California.

1995
Earthquake in northern Los Angeles kills 57.

2001
Energy crisis.

1800	1900	2000

1848
Gold discovered in California draws 80,000 prospectors in the 1849 gold rush.

1861–65
Civil War.

1869
Transcontinental Railroad completed.

1917–18
U.S. involvement in World War I.

1929
Stock market crash ushers in Great Depression.

1941–45
U.S. involvement in World War II.

1950–53
U.S. fights in the Korean War.

1964–73
U.S. involvement in Vietnam War.

2000
George W. Bush wins the closest presidential election in history.

2001
A terrorist attack in which four hijacked airliners crash into New York City's World Trade Center's Twin Towers, the Pentagon, and farmland in western Pennsylvania leaves thousands dead or injured.

▼ Nearly one hundred years ago, Long Beach, California, beckoned to swimmers and sunbathers.

Festivals and Fun For All

Check web site for exact date and directions.

Almond Festival, Oakley
Family fun abounds at this nutty festival.
www.oakleychamber.com/festival/funstuff.htm

Asparagus Festival, Stockton
This three-day, multi-event festival is held in San Joaquin County, the asparagus capital of the world.
www.asparagusfest.com

Cable Car Bell Ringing Competition, San Francisco
San Francisco gripmen compete against each other, clanging out tunes on cable car bells.
city.netmio.com/city/san_francisco/events/detail/1,1246,CI-ID357-LGen,00.html

California State Fair, Sacramento
Since 1954 the fair has showcased the talents and products of Californians.
www.bigfun.org

Chinese New Year Festival and Parade, San Francisco
The largest Chinese New Year celebration outside of Asia takes place in San Francisco's Chinatown. Decorated floats, marching bands, martial arts group, stilt walkers, lion dancers, and Chinese acrobatics enliven the parade, which is capped by a fireworks display.
www.chineseparade.com

Hollywood Film Festival, Hollywood
A four-day festival featuring new films.
www.hollywoodfilmfestival.com

Italian Street Painting Festival, San Rafael
San Rafael in Marin County re-creates a four hundred-year old Italian tradition. This festival, sponsored by the Youth in Arts, transforms the streets in front of the Mission San Rafael into a color-splashed asphalt gallery by hundreds of professional and student *madonnari* (street painters). Visitors can participate as well!
www.youthinarts.org/ispf.htm

The Napa Festival, Napa County
Folk, gospel, country, Cajun, Native American, Celtic, jazz, bluegrass, blues, Chicano, jug bands, and more rock this festival around the clock.
www.napfest.com

◄ Hollywood lit up at night.

Sacramento Arts Festival, Sacramento

This event features 225 contemporary craft and fine-art exhibitors, each selected through a jury system for the originality and quality of their work. The event is not only the premier art show in Sacramento but is also becoming one of the top art festivals in the country.

www.americanartfestivals.com/sac.html

San Diego Bay Bird Festival, San Diego

Family fun and educational activities explore the wealth of habitats, plants, and wildlife found in and around south San Diego Bay, the Tijuana Estuary, and the adjacent Pacific Ocean.

www.flite-tours.com/festival.htm

Swallows Day, San Juan Capistrano

Every summer the swallows migrate north to San Juan Capistrano to start new families. They remain until autumn and the swallows migrate south again. San Juan Capistrano celebrates this annual occurrence with a *mercado* (street fair) and a "Swallows Day" Parade.

www.sjc.net/fiesta/parade.html

The Tallships Festival, Dana Point

Watch as majestic tall ships sail into San Juan Bay. Nearby Dana Point (San Juan Bay) was once the site of a pirate raid, and the Port Royal Privateers are on hand to entertain the public by holding a mock trial, weddings, and historical reenactments that commemorate the event.

tallshipsfestival.com

◀ A tall ship under sail.

Books

Altman, Linda Jacobs. *The California Gold Rush in American History*. Springfield, NJ: Enslow Publishers, 1997. Find out how and why so many people rushed to California in the 1850s.

Brimner, Larry Dane. *A Migrant Family*. Minneapolis: Lerner Publications Company, 1992. The difficult lives of California's many migrant agricultural workers are portrayed.

Chippendale, Lisa A. *The San Francisco Earthquake of 1906*. New York: Chelsea House, 2000. The earthquake that shook San Francisco in 1906.

Howell, Judd. *Wildlife California*. San Francisco: Chronicle Books, 1991. The plants and animals of the Golden State.

Schwabacher, Martin. *The Chumash Indians*. New York: Chelsea House, 1995. Find out who lived in California before Europeans arrived.

Scott, Victoria, Ernest Jones, and Karen Lewis. *Sylvia Stark: A Pioneer*. Seattle: Open Hand Publishing, 1992. The true story of an African-American woman who traveled to California during the gold rush of the 1850s.

Stanley, Jerry. *Children of the Dust Bowl: The True Story of the School at Weedpatch Camp*. New York: Crown Publishers, 1992. The struggles of families from the "dust bowl" who traveled to California during the Great Depression in search of a better life.

Web Sites

▶ The official state web site
www.ca.gov/state/portal/myca_homepage.jsp

▶ The official web site of Sacramento, California's capital
www.sacramento.org/sacramento

▶ California Historical Society
www.calhist.org

▶ The American Memory Collection Finder: Search the Library of Congress for original material about California and the rest of the United States.
memory.loc.gov/ammem

Films and Documentaries

Boettcher, Steven, and Michael Trinklein. *Gold Rush*. Alexandria, VA: PBS/Wells Fargo Bank, 1998. Trinklein and Boettcher help viewers relive the quest for gold in frontier California.